TO

_____

FROM

_____

DATE

_____

HEALTHY, WEALTHY AND WISE

HEALTHY, WEALTHY AND WISE

Principals For Successful Living From The Life Of

BENJAMIN FRANKLIN

THE SUMMIT GROUP — FORT WORTH, TEXAS

THE SUMMIT GROUP
1227 West Magnolia, Suite 500, Fort Worth, Texas 76104

Page Design by Troy Reese

To Poor Richard, who in his life, was probably the Richest Richard in the Colonies. Not in money, mind you, but in the affections of a new and still wild country.

INTRODUCTION

Early America, the United States portion of it, had its George Washingtons, its Thomas Jeffersons, its Paul Reveres and assorted other heroes who have found their ways into the history books. But for a people still, in one sense of the word, too cognizant of princes, kings, queens, dictators and conquerors, Benjamin Franklin had to be a refreshingly new breeze of freedom, of good humor, of goodwill toward his fellow-man. He was clever enough to express it in his writings that quickly became the best sellers of his day and turned him from quite humble beginnings to a comfortable, useful and well-respected life.

Benjamin Franklin had a great love for his fellow Americans and for his struggling new country. He had a great rapport with the average man and the average woman of his day. One of the amazing things about his philosophy and about his thinking is that if he were a young author today, he would probably be as successful and as loved as he was in the eighteenth century.

That leads us to one explanation that must be made. Language usage, spelling, capitalization and punctuation have undergone many changes since Poor Richard published his annual almanacs, but we didn't dare change the charm of Ben's writing by attempting to update it. I call him "Ben" because, after spending many hours with him vicariously, one is sure that it is the way Ben would have wanted it.

Read him in good cheer as you sip your evening ale.

— The Editor

~ 1 ~

Early to bed and early to rise, makes a man
healthy, wealthy, and wise.

~ 2 ~

The way to be safe, is never to be secure.

~ 3 ~

Jack *Little* sow'd little, and little he'll reap.

~ 4 ~

He's a fool that makes his doctor his heir.

~ 5 ~

Great talkers, little doers.

~ 6 ~

Fear not Death; for the sooner we die,
the longer shall we be immortal.

~ 7 ~

Hunger never saw bad bread.

~ 8 ~

The favour of the Great is no inheritance.

~ 9 ~
Visits should be short, like a winters day,
Lest you're too troublesome hasten away.

~ 10 ~
Relation without friendship, friendship
without power, power without will, will without
effect, effect without profit, and profit without
virtue, are not worth a *farto*.

~ 11 ~
Fools make feasts and wise men eat 'em.

~ 12 ~

Ne'er take a wife till thou hast a house
(and a fire) to put her in.

~ 13 ~

Beware of the young doctor and the old barber.

~ 14 ~

He has chang'd his one ey'd horse for a blind one.

~ 15 ~

Eat to live, and not live to eat.

~ 16 ~

The poor have little, beggars none,
the rich too much, enough not one.

~ 17 ~

Beware of him that is slow to anger:
He is angry for something,
and will not be pleased for nothing.

~ 18 ~

He's gone, and forgot nothing but to say
Farewell—to his creditors.

~ 19 ~
Beware of meat twice boil'd,
and an old foe reconcil'd.

~ 20 ~
It is ill-manners to silence a fool,
and cruelty to let him go on.

~ 21 ~
He that pursues two hares at once,
does not catch one
and lets t'other go

~ 22 ~
To lengthen thy life, lessen thy meals.

~ 23 ~
Spare and have is better than *spend and crave.*

~ 24 ~
Laziness travels so slowly,
that *Poverty* soon overtakes him.

~ 25 ~
A fat kitchin, a lean will.

~ 26 ~
The Golden Age was never the present age.

~ 27 ~
Fish and visitors stink after three days.

~ 28 ~
Is there anything men take more pains about
than to make themselves unhappy?

~ 29 ~
Distrust and caution are the parents of security.

~ 30 ~
He is ill cloth'd, who is bare of virtue.

~ 31 ~
He that lies down with dogs,
shall rise up with fleas.

~ 32 ~
He that drinks fast, pays slow.

~ 33 ~
A good wife lost is God's gift lost.

~ 34 ~

Love your neighbor yet don't
pull down your hedge.

~ 35 ~

Old boys have their playthings as well as young
ones; the difference is only in the price.

~ 36 ~

The busy man has few idle Visitors;
to the boiling Pot
the Flies come not.

~ 37 ~
Take counsel in wine, but resolve
afterwards in water.

~ 38 ~
Tongue double, brings trouble.

~ 39 ~
Men and melons are hard to know.

~ 40 ~
There is no little enemy.

~ 41 ~

Half the truth is often a great lie.

~ 42 ~

Doors and walls are fools paper.

~ 43 ~

Keep your mouth wet, feet dry.

~ 44 ~

He's the best physician that knows
the worthlessness of most medicines.

~ 45 ~
A fine genius in his own country,
is like gold in the mine.

~ 46 ~
The heart of a fool is in his mouth, but the
mouth of a wise man is in his heart.

~ 47 ~
When knaves betray each other,
one can scarce be blamed,
or the other pitied.

~ 48 ~

He has lost his boots but sav'd his spurs.

~ 49 ~

Anoint a villain and he'll stab you,
stab him and he'll anoint you.

~ 50 ~

Where bread is wanting, all's to be sold.

~ 51 ~

Nothing more like a fool, than a drunken man.

~ 52 ~

There is neither honour nor gain
got in dealing with a villain.

~ 53 ~

Where carcasses are, eagles will gather,
And where good laws are,
much people flock thither.

~ 54 ~

God works wonders now and then;
Behold! a lawyer, an honest man!

~ 55 ~
Snowy winter, a plentiful harvest.

~ 56 ~
He that lives carnally, won't live eternally.

~ 57 ~
Innocence is its own defence.

~ 58 ~
Love, cough, and a smoke,
can't well be hid.

~ 59 ~
Without justice, courage is weak.

~ 60 ~
Would you live with ease,
Do what you ought, and not what you please.

~ 61 ~
Blame-all and *Praise-all* are two blockheads.

~ 62 ~
In success be moderate.

~ 63 ~

The wolf sheds his coat once a year;
his disposition never.

~ 64 ~

Don't think to hunt two hares with one dog.

~ 65 ~

Fools multiple folly.

~ 66 ~

Beauty and folly are old companions.

~ 67 ~
What one relishes, nourishes.

~ 68 ~
Many a man's own tongue gives evidence
against his understanding.

~ 69 ~
No man e'er was glorious, who was not laborious.

~ 70 ~
Better slip with foot than tongue.

~ 71 ~
Be not sick too late, nor well too soon.

~ 72 ~
Take this remark from *Richard* poor and lame,
Whate'er's begun in anger ends in shame.

~ 73 ~
Light purse, heavy heart.

~ 74 ~
Who pleasure gives, shall joy receive.

~ 75 ~
If you ride a horse, sit close and tight,
If you ride a man, sit easy and light.

~ 76 ~
Hope of gain,
Lessens pain.

~ 77 ~
Lawyers, Preachers, and Tomtits Eggs,
there are more of them hatch'd
than come to perfection.

~ 78 ~

Be neither silly, nor cunning, but wise.
Wedlock, as old men note, hath likened been,
Unto a publick crowd or common rout;
Where those that are without would fain get in,
And those that are within would fain get out.
Grief often treads upon the heels of pleasure,
Marry'd in haste, we oft repent at leisure;
Some by experience find these words misplac'd,
Marry'd at leisure, they repent in haste.

~ 79 ~
Where there's marriage without love,
there will be love without marriage.

~ 80 ~
All things are cheap to the saving,
dear to the wasteful.

~ 81 ~
Would you persuade,
speak of interest, not of reason.

~ 82 ~
Happy's the wooing that's not long a doing.

~ 83 ~
You may delay, but *Time* will not.

~ 84 ~
There have been as great souls unknown to fame as any of the most famous.

~ 85 ~
Drive thy Business! —let not it drive you.

~ 86 ~
He that cannot obey, cannot command.

~ 87 ~
Teach your child to hold his tongue,
he'll learn fast enough to speak.

~ 88 ~
A good man is seldom uneasy, an ill one never easy.

~ 89 ~
An Egg today is better than a Hen tomorrow.

~ 90 ~
Do good to thy friend to keep him,
to thy enemy to gain him.

~ 91 ~
Onions can make ev'n heirs and widows weep.

~ 92 ~
He does not possess wealth, it possesses him.

~ 93 ~
Approve not of him who commends all you say.

~ 94 ~

Don't value a man for the quality he is of,
but the qualities he possesses.

~ 95 ~

An innocent *Plowman* is more worthy
than a vicious *Prince*.

~ 96 ~

He that is rich need not live sparingly,
and he that can live sparingly
need not be rich.

~ 97 ~

If you wou'd be reveng'd of your enemy,
govern yourself.

~ 98 ~

Drink water, put the money in your pocket, and
leave the *Dry-bellyach* in the *Punchbowl*.

~ 99 ~

Plough deep, while sluggards sleep;
And you shall have corn, to sell and keep.

~ 100 ~
Strange, that he who lives by shifts,
and seldom shifts himself.

~ 101 ~
As sore places meet most rubs,
proud folks meet most affronts.

~ 102 ~
He that waits upon fortune,
is never sure of a dinner.

~ 103 ~
A learned blockhead is a greater blockhead
than an ignorant one.

~ 104 ~
A wise man will desire no more,
than what he may get justly, use soberly,
distribute cheerfully, and leave contentedly.

~ 105 ~
Most fools think
they are only ignorant.

~ 106 ~
Avarice and Happiness never saw each other,
how then shou'd they become acquainted.

~ 107 ~
Look before, or you'll find yourself behind.

~ 108 ~
The family of fools is ancient.

~ 109 ~
Necessity never made a good bargain.

~ 110 ~

If you would have guests merry with your cheer,
Be so your self, or so at least appear.

~ 111 ~

Pain wastes the Body,
Pleasures the understanding.

~ 112 ~

Bad commentators spoil the best of books
So God sends meat (they say) the devil cooks.

~ 113 ~
By diligence and patience,
the mouse bit in to the cable.

~ 114 ~
He that best understands the world,
least likes it.

~ 115 ~
There's many witty men
whose brains can't fill their bellies.

~ 116 ~
Sampson with his *strong body*,
had a *weak head,* or he would not have
laid it in a harlot's lap.

~ 117 ~
Keep thy shop, and thy shop will keep thee.

~ 118 ~
Be civil to *all*; serviceable to *many*;
familiar with *few*;
Friend to *one*; Enemy to *none*.

~ 119 ~
Nothing but money,
Is sweeter than honey.

~ 120 ~
Humility makes great men twice honourable.

~ 121 ~
A lie stands on one leg, Truth on two.

~ 122 ~
It is better to take many injuries than to give one.

~ 123 ~

A man is never so ridiculous by those qualitites
that are his own as by those that he affects to have.

~ 124 ~

Laws *too gentle* are seldom *obeyed*;
too severe, seldom *executed*.

~ 125 ~

Silence is not always a sign of wisdom,
but babbling is ever a mark of folly.

~ 126 ~
Here comes the orator! with his flood of words,
and his drop of reason.

~ 127 ~
Sal laughs at every thing you say.
Why? Because she has fine teeth.

~ 128 ~
If what most men admire, they would despise,
'Twould look as if mankind were growing wise.

~ 129 ~
The COURTS

When Popery in *Britain* sway'd, I've read,
The lawyers fear'd they should be
damn'd when dead,
Because they had no saint to hand their pray'rs,
And in heav'n's court take care of their affairs.
Therefore consulting, *Evanus* they sent
To *Rome* with a huge purse, on this intent
That to the Holy Father making known
Their woeful case, he might appoint them one.

Being arriv'd he offers his complaint
In language smooth, and humbly begs a saint:
For why, says he, when other in heav'n wou'd call,
Physicians, seamen, scholars, tradesman, all
Have their own saints, we *Lawyers* none at all.
The Pope was puzzel'd, never puzzel'd worse
For with pleas'd eyes he saw the proffer'd purse
But ne'er, in all his knowledge or his reading,
He'd met with one good man that
practis'd pleading;
Who then should be the Saint? He could not tell.
At length the thing was thus concluded well.

Within our city, says his holiness,
There is one church fill'd with the images
Of all the saints, with whom the wall's surrounded,
Blindfold *Evanus*, lead him three times round it,
Then let him feel (*but give me first the purse*)
And take the first he finds, for better or worse.
Round went *Evanus* till he came where stood
St. Michael with the Devil under's foot;
And groping round, he seiz'd old Satan's head,
This be our Saint, he cries: Amen, the Father said.
But when they open'd poor Evanus' *eyes,*
Alack! he sunk with shame and with surprize!

~ 130 ~
If you know how to spend less than you get,
you have the Philosophers-Stone.

~ 131 ~
In a discreet man's mouth,
a publick thing is private.

~ 132 ~
Are you angry that others disappoint you?
Remember you cannot depend
upon yourself.

~ 133 ~
An old young man, will be a young old man.

~ 134 ~
Haste makes waste.

~ 135 ~
Diligence is the mother of good-luck.

~ 136 ~
None preaches better than the ant,
and she says nothing.

~ 137 ~
Do not do that which you would not have known.

~ 138 ~
Don't throw stones at your neighbours,
if your own windows are glass.

~ 139 ~
Wealth is not his that has it, but his that enjoys it.

~ 140 ~
'Tis easy to see, hard to foresee.

~ 141 ~
Keep flax from fire, youth from gaming.

~ 142 ~
He that sells upon trust, loses many friends,
and always wants money.

~ 143 ~
There's more old drunkards than old doctors.

~ 144 ~
He that can have patience, can have what he will.

~ 145 ~
Whimsical *Will* once fancy'd he was ill,
The doctor's call'd, who thus examin'd *Will*;
How is your Appetite? O, as to that
I eat right heartily, you see I'm fat.
How is your Sleep anights?
'Tis sound and good;
I eat, drink, sleep as well as e'er I cou'd.
Well, says the doctor, clapping on his hat;
I'll give you something shall remove all that.

~ 146 ~
God helps them that help themselves.

~ 147 ~
The rotten apple spoils his companion.

~ 148 ~
He that speaks much, is much mistaken.

~ 149 ~
He that would live in peace and at ease,
Must not speak all he knows, nor judge all he sees.

~ 150 ~
Creditors have better memories than debtors.

~ 151 ~
He that scatters thorns, let him not go barefoot.

~ 152 ~
God heals, and the doctor takes the fees.

~ 153 ~
If you desire many things,
many things will seem but a few.

~ 154 ~
COURTS

For gratitude there's none exceed 'em,
(Their clients know this when they bleed 'em).
Since they who give most for their laws,
Have most return'd, and carry th' cause.
All know, except an arrant Tony,
That Right and Wrong's meer ceremony.
It is enough that the law jargon,
Gives the best bidder the best bargain.

~ 155 ~
Mary's mouth costs her nothing, for she never
opens it but at others expense.

~ 156 ~
The use of money is all the advantage there is
in having money.

~ 157 ~
Light purse, heavy heart.

~ 158 ~

A countryman between two lawyers,
is like a fish between two cats.

~ 159 ~

He that can take rest is greater
than he that can take cities.

~ 160 ~

He that can compose himself,
is wiser than he that composes books.

~ 161 ~
A false friend and a shadow,
attend only while the sun shines.

~ 162 ~
After crosses and losses
men grow humbler and wiser.

~ 163 ~
At the working man's house hunger looks in
but dares not enter.

~ 164 ~

On his death-bed poor *Lubin* lies;
His spouse is in despair;
With frequent sobs, and mutual cries,
They both express their care.
A diff'rent cause, says Parson *Sly,*
The same effect may give;
Poor *Lubin* fears that he shall die;
His wife, that he may live.

~ 165 ~

Never spare the Parson's wine,
nor the Baker's pudding.

~ 166 ~
Well done is better than well said.

~ 167 ~
The worst wheel of the cart makes the most noise.

~ 168 ~
Don't misinform your doctor nor your lawyer.

~ 169 ~
To whom thy secret thou dost tell,
To him thy freedom thou dost sell.

~ 170 ~

Jack's wife was born in *Wiltshire*, brought up in
Cumberland, led much of
her life in *Bedfordshire*, sent her husband into
Huntingdonshire in order to bring him into
Buckinghamshire: But he took courage in
Hartfordshire, and carry'd her into *Staffordshire*,
or else he might have liv'd and dy'd in *Shrewsbury*.

~ 171 ~

Sell not virtue to purchase wealth,
nor liberty to purchase power.

~ 172 ~
Time is an herb that cures all diseases.

~ 173 ~
Who has deceiv'd thee so oft as thy self?

~ 174 ~
Great talkers should be cropt,
for they've no need of ears.

~ 175 ~
Let thy vices die before thee.

~ 176 ~

The ancients tell us what is best; but we must
learn of the moderns what is fittest.

~ 177 ~

Since thou art not sure of a minute,
throw not away an hour.

~ 178 ~

Keep your eyes wide open before marriage,
half shut afterwards.

~ 179 ~
As we must account for every idle word,
so we must for every idle silence.

~ 180 ~
Reading makes a full man, meditation
a profound man, discourse a clear man.

~ 181 ~
There is much difference between imitating a
good man, and counterfeiting him.

~ 182 ~

Search others for their virtues,
thy self for thy vices.

~ 183 ~

Each year one vicious habit rooted out,
In time might make the worst man
good throughout.

~ 184 ~

Wink at small faults;
remember thou has great ones.

~ 185 ~
Wish a miser long life, and you wish him no good.

~ 186 ~
Eat to please thyself, but dress to please others.

~ 187 ~
Trust thyself and another shall not betray thee.

~ 188 ~
Let thy child's first lesson be obedience,
and the second will be what thou wilt.

~ 189 ~

Historians relate, not so much what is done,
as what they would have believed.

~ 190 ~

He that falls in love with himself,
will have no rivals.

~ 191 ~

Blessed is he that expects nothing,
for he shall never be disappointed.

~ 192 ~

He that pays for work before it's done,
has but a pennyworth for twopence.

~ 193 ~

Thou canst not joke an enemy into a friend;
but thou may'st a friend into an enemy.

~ 194 ~

Sin is not hurtful because it is forbidden
but it is forbidden because it's hurtful.

~ 195 ~

To bear other peoples afflictions,
every one has courage enough,
and to spare.

~ 196 ~

A change of *Fortune* hurts a wise man no more
than a change of the *Moon*.

~ 197 ~

He that riseth late must trot all day, and shall
scarce overtake his business at night.

~ 198 ~
Industry need not wish.

~ 199~
An empty bag cannot stand upright.

~ 200 ~
Happy that nation, fortunate that age,
whose history is not diverting.

~ 201 ~
None are deceived but they that confide.

~ 202 ~
Man's tongue is soft, and bone doth lack;
Yet a stroke therewith may break a man's back.
There are lazy minds as well as lazy bodies.

~ 203 ~
A house without woman and firelight,
is like a body without soul or sprite.

~ 204 ~
You can bear your own faults,
and why not a fault in your wife?

~ 205 ~

Who says Jack is not generous? he is always
fond of giving, and cares not for receiving-
What? Why; Advice.

~ 206 ~

Learn of the skillful: He that teaches himself,
hath a fool for his master.

~ 207 ~

If you would keep your secret from an enemy,
tell it not to a friend.

~ 208 ~
Have you some what to do to-morrow, do it to-day.

~ 209 ~
Ill customs and bad advice are seldom forgotten.

~ 210 ~
Experience keeps a dear school,
yet fools will learn in no other.

~ 211 ~
Death take no bribes.

~ 212 ~
Industry, perseverance, and frugality,
make fortune yield.

~ 213 ~
Give me yesterday's bread, this day's flesh,
and last year's cyder.

~ 214 ~
How few there are who have courage enough
to own their own faults,
or resolution enough to mend them!

~ 215 ~

Eat few suppers, and you'll need few medicines.

~ 216 ~

Who is strong? He that can conquer his bad habits.

~ 217 ~

Who is rich? He that rejoices in his portion.

~ 218 ~

Beware of little expences,
a small leak will sink a great ship.

~ 219 ~

Two trav'ling beggars, (I've forgot their names)
An oyster found to which they both laid claim.
Warm the dispute! At length to law they'd go,
As richer fools for trifles often do.
The cause two petty-foggers undertake,
Resolving right or wrong some gain to make.
They jangle till the court this judgment gave,
Determining what every one should have.
Blind plaintiff, lame defendant, share
The friendly law's impartial care:
A shell for him, a shell for thee;
The MIDDLE'S bench and lawyer's fee.

~ 220 ~
Old young and old long.

~ 221 ~
He who buys had need have one hundred eyes,
but one's enough for him that sells the stuff.

~ 222 ~
Wars bring scars.

~ 223 ~
He's a fool that cannot conceal his wisdom.

~ 224 ~

Make haste slowly.

"I'll warrant ye" goes before *Rashness*.

Who'd-a-tho't it? comes sneaking after.

~ 225 ~

Hear *Reason*, or she'll make you feel her.

~ 226 ~

To God we owe fear and love;

to our neighbors justice and charity;

to our selves prudence and sobriety.

~ 227 ~
Vanity backbites more than *Malice*.

~ 228 ~
You may talk too much on the best of subjects.

~ 229 ~
Idleness is the greatest prodigality.

~ 230 ~
There are no fools so troublesome
as those that have wit.

~ 231 ~
Many complain of their memory,
few of their judgment.

~ 232 ~
He that would travel much, should eat little.

~ 233 ~
A quarrelsome man has no good neighbours.

~ 234 ~
God gives all things to industry.

~ 235 ~

One man may be more cunning than another,
but not more cunning than every body else.

~ 236 ~

'Tis easier to prevent bad habits
than to break them.

~ 237 ~

The ancients tell us what is best; but we must
learn of the moderns what is fittest.

~ 238 ~
Interest which blinds some people,
enlightens others.

~ 239 ~
He that resolves to mend hereafter,
resolves not to mend now.

~ 240 ~
It's the easiest thing in the world
for a man to deceive himself.

~ 241 ~
Want of care does us more damage
than want of knowledge.

~ 242 ~
Take courage, mortal;
Death can't banish thee out of the universe.

~ 243 ~
Can wealth give happiness?
Look round and see,
What gay distress! What splindid misery!

~ 244 ~
The sting of a reproach, is the truth of it.

~ 245 ~
There is no man so bad,
but he secretly respects the good.

~ 246 ~
A good example is the best sermon.

~ 247 ~
A Mob's a monster; Heads aplenty, but no brains.

~ 248 ~

We are not so sensible to the greatest health
as of the least sickness.

~ 249 ~

Liberality is not giving much but giving wisely.

~ 250 ~

If your head is wax, don't walk in the sun.

~ 251 ~

Wealth and content are not always bed-fellows.

~ 252 ~
Clean your finger, before you point at my spots.

~ 253 ~
All would live long, but none would be old.

~ 254 ~
Wise men learn by others harms;
fools by their own.

~ 255 ~
Most of the learning in use, is of no great use.

~ 256 ~
Words may shew a man's Wit,
but *Actions* his meaning.

~ 257 ~
Having been poor is no shame,
but being ashamed of it, is.

~ 258 ~
Declaiming against pride,
is not always a sign of humility.

~ 259 ~
Great good-nature, without prudence,
is a great misfortune.

~ 260 ~
He is a governor that governs his passions,
and he a servant that serves them.

~ 261 ~
If it were not for the belly,
the back might wear gold.

~ 262 ~
Wouldst thou confound thine enemy,
be good thy self.

~ 263 ~
Many a man thinks he is buying pleasure,
when he is really selling himself a slave to it.

~ 264 ~
He that spills the rum, loses that only; He that
drinks it, often loses both that and himself.

~ 265 ~
Being ignorant is not so much a shame,
as being unwilling to learn.

~ 266 ~
Do not squander time,
for that's what life is made of.

~ 267 ~
Little strokes,
Fell great oaks.

~ 268 ~

Genius without education is like silver in the mine.
So ignorant, that he bought a cow to ride on.

~ 269 ~

Hide not your talents, they for use were made.
What's a sun-dial in the shade!

~ 270 ~

What signifies knowing the names,
if you know not the natures of things.

~ 271 ~
The doors of wisdom are never shut.

~ 272 ~
Most people return small favours,
acknowledge middling ones,
and repay great ones with ingratitude.

~ 273 ~
Many a man would have been worse,
if his estate had been better.

~ 274 ~
Many have quarrel'd about religion,
that never practised it.

~ 275 ~
Fond pride of dress is sure an empty curse;
E're *Fancy* you consult, consult your purse.

~ 276 ~
Don't judge men's wealth or piety,
by their *Sunday* appearances.

~ 277 ~
Friendship increases by visiting friends,
but by visiting seldom.

~ 278 ~
Great estates may venture more;
Little boats must keep near shore.

~ 279 ~
If worldly goods cannot save me from death,
they ought not to hinder me of eternal life.

~ 280 ~
Not to oversee workmen,
is to leave your purse open.

~ 281 ~
We may give advice, but we cannot give conduct.

~ 282 ~
To-day is Yesterday's pupil.

~ 283 ~
The wise and brave dares own that he was wrong.

~ 284 ~
If your riches are yours,
why don't you take them with you
to the t'other world?

~ 285 ~
Kings and Bears
often worry their keepers.

~ 286 ~
A brother may not be a friend,
but a friend will always be a brother.

~ 287 ~

'Tis more noble to forgive,
and more manly to despise,
than to revenge an injury.

~ 288 ~

If man could have half his wishes,
he would double his troubles.

~ 289 ~

Hold your council before dinner;
the full belly hates thinking as well as acting.

~ 290 ~
The proud hate pride—in others.

~ 291 ~
Who judges best of a man, his enemies or himself?

~ 292 ~
Drink does not drown care, but waters it,
and makes it grow fast.

~ 293 ~
Meanness is the parent of insolence.

~ 294 ~

For want of a nail the shoe is lost;
for want of a shoe, the horse is lost;
for want of a horse the rider is lost.

~ 295 ~

A temper to bear much, will have much to bear.

~ 296 ~

'Tis against some mens principle to pay interest,
and seems against others interest
to pay the principal.

~ 297 ~
Success has ruin'd many a man.

~ 298 ~
A great talker may be no fool,
but he is one that relies on him.

~ 299 ~
Paintings and fightings are best seen at a distance.

~ 300 ~
It is not leisure that is not used.

~ 301 ~
When reason preaches,
if you won't hear her she'll box your ears.

~ 302 ~
He that is of opinion money will do every thing,
may well be suspected
of doing every thing for money.

~ 303 ~
If you would reap praise you must sow the seeds,
Gentle words and useful deeds.

~ 304 ~
Ignorance leads men into a party,
and *Shame* keeps them from getting out again.

~ 305 ~
He that best understands the world, least likes it.

~ 306 ~
An ill wound, but not an ill name, may be healed.

~ 307 ~
A lean award is better than a fat judgment.

~ 308 ~
Anger is never without a reason,
but seldom with a good one.

~ 309 ~
When out of favour, none know thee; when in,
thou dost not know thyself.

~ 310 ~
He that builds before he counts the cost,
acts foolishly; and he that counts before he
builds, finds he did not count wisely.

~ 311 ~
Take heed of the vinegar of sweet wine,
and the anger of good-nature.

~ 312 ~
If you have no honey in your pot,
have some in your mouth.

~ 313 ~
Serving God is doing good to man,
but praying is thought an easier service,
and therefore more generally chosen.

~ 314 ~
Be slow in choosing a friend, slower in changing.

~ 315 ~
The discontented man finds no easy chair.

~ 316 ~
Gifts much expected, are *paid*, not *given*.

~ 317 ~
He that doth what he should not,
shall feel what he would not.

~ 318 ~
In the affairs of this world men are saved,
not by faith, but by the want of it.

~ 319 ~
The learned fool writes his nonsense in better
language than the unlearned;
but still 'tis nonsense.

~ 320 ~
If you'd know the value of money,
go and borrow some.

~ 321 ~
The cat in gloves catches no mice.

~ 322 ~
Two dry sticks will burn a green one.

~ 323 ~
There was never a good knife made of bad steel.

~ 324 ~
March windy, and April rainy,
makes May the pleasantest month of any.

~ 325 ~
Bad gains are truly losses.

~ 326 ~
Nothing dries sooner than a tear.

~ 327 ~
Men take more pains to mask than mend.

~ 328 ~
Reader, farewell, all happiness attend thee:
May each *New Year* better and richer find thee.

~ 329 ~

Franklin's Epitaph (self-written in 1728)
The body of B. Franklin,
Printer;
Like the cover of an old book,
Its contents torn out,
And stript of its lettering and gilding,
Lies here, food for worms.
But the work shall not be wholly lost:
For it will, as he believ'd, appear once more,
In a new and more perfect edition,
Corrected and amended
By the author.

He was Born Jan. 6. 1706
Died 17__
The date (*and Franklin was good with the stars
and predicted lots of other things*), either he did
not
properly foresee or chose not to divulge.
Franklin would depart this vale of tears in 1790,
which chronologically rendered him
84 productive years.